THE AUSTIN SEVEN
a pictorial tribute

CONNOISSEUR CARBOOK **1**

The
Austin Seven

A PICTORIAL TRIBUTE by R. J. WYATT

MRP MOTOR RACING PUBLICATIONS

A CONNOISSEUR CARBOOK
published by
MOTOR RACING PUBLICATIONS LTD
56 Fitzjames Avenue, Croydon, Surrey, CR0 5DD

First published 1975
ISBN 0 900549 26 2

Printed in Great Britain by TeamPrint, London EC1

Contents

Sir Herbert Austin. A photograph taken about the time of his work on the design of the first Austin Seven, around 1920.

The Austin Seven

"I'd rather have given the world the Austin Seven, my dear fellow, than have won the Gordon-Bennett race for England a dozen times over, and in twelve consecutive years. Hang it, you don't realise what Austin has done. I wonder, indeed, if Austin himself realises what he has done? Ford had a unique market, on his own doorstep, for the Model T, one which had never existed previously and will never exist again. Austin had not. Austin's case was an instance of that very uncommon phenomena, a supply creating a demand, and filling it to the last ounce and penny piece." — S.F. Edge, 1925.

That, from a man of S.F. Edge's calibre, was a compliment indeed. It sums up Herbert Austin's greatest achievement, the design and production of a new and unusual car at a time when very few other manufacturers would have dared to take the risk. Austin's previous engineering designs were conventional. When he did move into new fields, more often than not the theory was good, but the practice poor. As an example, in 1913 he worked out a clever double drive propeller shaft for the 2-3 ton lorry in which shafts took the drive obliquely to each rear wheel, but the complications were such that it was impossible to keep the bevels in correct adjustment. The theory was brilliant, but the system did not work.

Austin was born in 1866, and spent his early years in Australia as an engineer responsible for sheep-shearing machinery sold by the Wolseley Sheep-Shearing Machine Company. In the late 1880's he returned to England and set about designing a car of his own. His first prototype was a three-wheeler, but in 1899 came his first production Wolseley, a sturdy and reliable car with four wheels and a single-cylinder horizontal engine. Austin would not entertain the vertical engine, but after a dispute with the Wolseley Company in 1905 he left to form the Austin Motor Company at Longbridge with money borrowed from Frank Kayser of the Kayser-Ellison Steel Company. His first car had a vertical engine!

7

The story of how Austin and one of his junior draughtsmen, Stanley Edge, worked on several preliminary sketches for a new concept of a small car at the billiard table at Austin's home, Lickey Grange, has become legend, and it was from those hesitant beginnings that the most successful car of the 1920's grew. It created its own market because it was efficient, economical and reliable, but it had some other quality which is less easy to define. As it created its own market, it did so amongst a class who regarded the car as being reserved for the more wealthy. Those who bought Austin Sevens thought of them as more than just a means of transport. They were treasured, undreamed of possessions — members of the family.

In the first year of production, to October 1923, 1934 cars and 2 chassis were produced. By 1926, the figure had reached 14,000 and it exceeded 20,000 each year until 1937, the greatest numbers being made in 1929 (26,447) and 1935 (27,280). By 1939, when the Seven was replaced by the Big Seven, over 300,000 had been sold, excluding those made under licence in America, Japan, France and Germany.

In the early 1930's, it was possible to buy a new Austin Seven for a little more than £100. With running costs at a penny a mile a new section of the population was able to take to the roads. Other manufacturers followed suit with small cars, the Morris Minor and Clyno Nine being amongst the most popular and, later on, the Ford Eight. The motor manufacturing industry, with this vast, previously untapped market at its disposal, grew in strength to become the major British industrial activity, an essential part of the British economy, and a prime export earner.

The early attempts to ridicule the "motorised pram" or "soap-box on wheels" all seem to have re-bounded. They became terms of endearment rather than ridicule. Then, to beat everything, people started to win races in them.

E.C. Gordon England was perhaps the first person to advocate a racing career for the new miniature car. Austin had been involved in motor trials and races from the beginning, including the 1,000-miles trial and various Gordon-Bennett and Grand Prix races until 1908, after which he was content to prepare Austin cars for his wealthy customers to use. In 1921, he allowed a special Twenty hp racer to be built in the factory for his son-in-law, Arthur Waite, who soon became interested in the prospect of a Seven racer. A car was ready shortly after the new production model was introduced, and it was taken to Brooklands for the Easter Monday meeting on March 23rd, 1923, when it covered a flying lap at 62.64 mph. During the following month Waite took the car to Monza for the Cycle-car Grand Prix and won the 750 cc class handsomely. It was the beginning of a success story which was to continue right through to World War Two and even to embrace a team of sophisticated single-seaters with twin-overhead-camshaft engines.

Having passed rather ignominiously through the hands of the special-builders (the first Lotus was in fact a modified Austin) just before and after the war, surviving Sevens have since taken on a new lease of life amongst Vintage and Post-Vintage car enthusiasts. Today, thousands of pounds are spent building replicas of sports and racing Sevens, and even more on the restoration of cars to their original condition.

The Austin Seven did not die. The enjoyment which it gave to an earlier generation has been repeated, and no doubt, it will continue to give pleasure to many more enthusiasts in the future.

Some of the illustrations featured in this book have appeared elsewhere over the years. To have excluded them would have been a mistake because, familiar though they may be to some devotees, they fulfil an important function in helping to trace the development of the car; without them, this pictorial tribute would have done less than justice to a great car.

ACKNOWLEDGEMENTS

Most of the illustrations in this book are from my own collection, and have been accumulated over the years from Ron Beach, the last head of photography at the Austin factory in Birmingham, from the files of the now defunct Austin Magazine, and from old members of the staff at Austin's, to all of whom I am most grateful.

The proprietors of PUNCH kindly gave me permission to reproduce the cartoons which once enlivened the pages of their excellent magazine.

The Austin winged-wheel trademark and the familiar script.

An early concept

Predecessor to the Austin Seven. During a period when Austin was concentrating on a range of cars with engines from 18 to 50 horsepower, and his 15-hp model was regarded as 'light', he also produced a few 7-hp cars with a 105 x 127mm single-cylinder engine. They were available in 1910 and 1911, but production was taken over by the Swift Company in Coventry.

Seventeen years of Sevens

Sir Herbert Austin at the wheel of the prototype Seven in its earliest form. The small screen had no provision for the retention of the hood, and oil lamps and a hand klaxon were fitted, presumably before the car had been wired for electric lights.

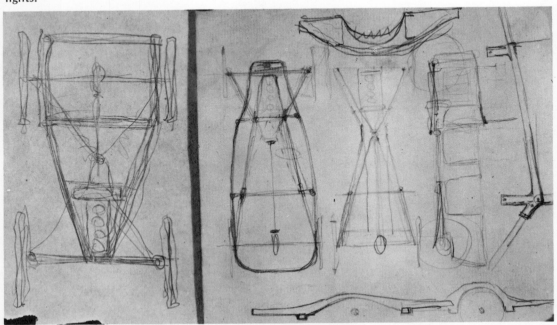

A page from Austin's sketch book, showing the first rough drawings he made of the frame and layout. Both the cruciform and A-shaped frames were considered, the final thoughts being shown in the sketch on the left.

Another very early car, this time with the production windscreen and electric lamps. The lack of running boards was a distinguishing feature of the earliest Sevens.

Running boards added, but still with the stepped panel in the scuttle sides; this photograph was used as a Press handout in 1923.

THE DRIVER. "What do you think of those little things?"
THE PASSENGER. "Make topping ash-trays."

One of the earliest cars, now preserved in the Birmingham Science Museum. The interior door catch can be seen on the passenger's side.

14

Above: This picture of OL 166, one of the first Austin Sevens, was taken early in 1923 for issue to the Press, although for some reason it was not used at that time. Below: Evidently taken at the same time, and with the same girls, this is a mystery Seven, featuring four-stud disc wheels and a strange body, which seems to have disappeared almost as soon as it was made.

Two views of a 1923 car, OK 9365, one showing the limit of the carrying capacity of the rear compartment. The catalogue stated: "The space at the back of the driver's seat has intentionally been restricted so that any attempt to overload the car with too many passengers will be militated against by the discomfort attached thereto"!

"Ample room in the rear for luggage or for the family." Presumably this advertising slogan referred only to families consisting of small children or legless midgets.

A 1923 Seven with hood and side screens erected; the screens were not very effective and were seldom used.

This comfortably settled old gentleman was 81 when he posed for this Press picture. The attachment fixed to the top of the steering wheel could be a watch, or even a compass.

A happy face often seen in Austin Press pictures was that of Jack Gethins, Austin's chauffeur, who lived beyond his 90th birthday. This car has a stepped scuttle and interior door catches, but is fitted with the perpendicular screen. Austin never liked the sloping screen and he did away with it as soon as the Seven began to be produced in quantity.

It was decided that something had to be shown at the Commercial Motor Show in 1923, and the result was this single-seater taxicab. It is doubtful if any more were made.

The Austin Seven

Features:
4-cylinder Engine.
Water Cooled.
Detachable Head.
Automatic Lubrication.
Three-speed Gearbox.
Bevel Drive.   Differential.
Brakes on all Wheels.

Equipment:
Electric Lighting.
Electric Horn.
Hood and Double Screen.
Side Curtains.
Spare Wheel and Tyre.

Price at **£165** Works

Write for "The Motor for the Million,"
—a delightful booklet illustrated.—

THE AUSTIN MOTOR CO. LTD.
NORTHFIELD, BIRMINGHAM,
And 479-483, OXFORD STREET, London, W.1.

This advertising material seen in March, 1923, was typical of the period.

By 1926, when this photograph was taken at Longbridge, the "Chummy" was firmly established in its most familiar form. About 10,000 of them were made that year.

This experimental fixed-head coupe was made in March, 1926, but the demand for such a body was very limited.

"Nothing serious, dear. Got run over by a horse."

Fabric, or "rag" bodies were introduced in 1927. A wooden framework was covered with canvas, padding and fabric, the object being to produce a body free from rattles and drumming. By 1930, the fabric phase had passed, but in 1929, at the height of their popularity, over 8000 fabric-bodied Sevens were sold.

A fabric model of October, 1928, on which a single-piece windscreen was adopted for better visibility. This example had wider doors than on earlier saloons, and was known as the "Widoor".

This coupe, again with the wide door, was exhibited at the 1928 Motor Show in London, after which it was sent to America to be seen at the New York Show in 1929. Production was relatively small — 51 cars were built in 1928, 347 in 1929, 128 in 1930 and only seven in 1931.

"I can't come out yet, dear; I'm washing the baby."

More popular than the fabric-bodied car was the metal saloon — the "Top Hat". This example was made in August, 1928, and is preserved in the Lucerne Museum of Transport.

A specially prepared 1928/29 works demonstration chassis.

The two-seater tourer of September, 1929. Only 107 of this model were made that year, and in its best year, 1934, production was only just over 1000 cars.

By far the most popular Austin Seven model in 1929 was this standard tourer, of which no less than 8253 were made that year.

BUS-DRIVER (*to small car cutting-in*). "An' 'oo might you think you wos? The flying squad?"

Professional strong man, impatient when traffic signals are against him, resolves himself into a pedestrian.

July, 1930, and nearing the end of the production life of the fabric saloon. Only about 800 of this model were produced.

By 1931 the internal dimensions of the body had been increased. Refinements such as trafficators and a louvred bonnet were added, and for the first time the rear compartment could take two adult passengers in reasonable comfort.

Austin Sevens became jewels in 1933. This was the Opal two-seater, which was to be followed later by the famous Ruby saloon and eventually by the Pearl cabriolet. By now, Sir Herbert had relented (very slightly!) with the slope of the windscreens.

August, 1934, and the first of the elegant Ruby saloons, with such modern refinements as bumpers, recessed trafficators, opening bonnet louvres and a cowelled radiator.

A 1933 tourer with well-tailored hood and side screens that went a long way towards keeping out the wind and rain.

The Ruby of 1936/37 in its final form. Although Austin Seven production had hit its peak figure of 27,280 in 1935, annual output was still in excess of 23,000, of which the great majority were Ruby saloons.

The Pearl cabriolet of January, 1937, the car which combined the advantages of a saloon and a tourer. Production was limited to around 1000 cars per year.

Special-bodied Sevens

Specialist body-builders were quick to adapt the Austin Seven chassis. Late in 1924, Wilson Motors of London offered this Burghley Sports model in dark grey with scarlet wings.

A contemporary of the Burghley Sports, this delightful little car with a polished aluminium body was produced by Hughes of Birmingham.

E. C. Gordon England, who raced Austins, also owned a coachbuilding firm. This is one of his famous Cup model Sevens climbing Beggar's Roost in the summer of 1927.

A later example of a Gordon England model, dated 1929.

The Gordon England Sunshine saloon of 1928. Note the cross-bracing of the roof.

Fabric bodies were a Gordon England speciality. They were cheap to produce, without the necessity for expensive panel-beating or the provision of press machines. This example dates from 1929.

Before settling down to make SS Jaguar cars in the 1930's, William Lyons built bodies for Austin Sevens and other chassis. This 1931 Austin Swallow is a typically stylish example of his company's work.

Featuring a body specially built by Austin's themselves, the Austin Seven Military Model, of 1934, was used by the cavalry for scouting.

Sevens under licence

Thousands of Sevens were built overseas under licence. Most of them were given names and characters to suit local fashions, but the chassis parts mostly were identical to those of the British cars. This is a Rosengart, made in France in 1928, in which a sideways-facing rear seat turned the car into a three-seater.

Even the Americans made a copy of it, this Bantam, dating from 1930, having a distinctly transatlantic appearance.

The German adaptation was the Dixi, production of which followed an agreement signed in 1927.

This German Dixi Sports of 1930 has been restored by an enthusiast.

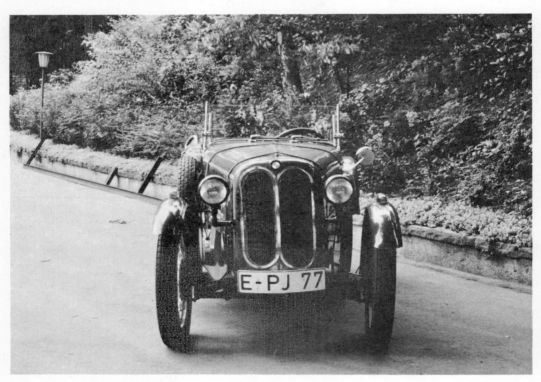

The racing Sevens

So many different Austin Sevens were used for motor racing that it would be impossible to illustrate all the variations, but a start must be made with Capt Arthur Waite and Alf Depper (car number 3) waiting on the line before the Monza race in 1923.

Sir Herbert with the first Austin Seven racing team at the Boulogne meeting in August, 1923.

Capt Waite in one of the Boulogne cars on the day that he won the Easter small-car handicap at Brooklands in 1923.

Waite entered for the 750 cc class of the 1924 Grand Prix des Voiturettes at Le Mans and took third place.

One of the first supercharged Austin Seven engines. The blower fed to a Cox-Atmos carburettor and helped the engine to develop 36 bhp at 5000 rpm.

A successful Gordon England Cup model, in which P. Brough won the disabled drivers' handicap race at Brooklands in April, 1926.

Capt Samuelson in Gordon England's 200-miles race car, after winning a race at Brooklands in the spring of 1926.

J. P. Dingle overtaking to win a 150-miles race at Brooklands in August, 1927.

Record-breaking at Montlhéry in June, 1928. H. B. Parker taking over from C. K. Chase whilst breaking the 24-hours record. Approximately 1584 miles were covered in the time, giving a magnificent average speed, including stops, of 65.98 mph.

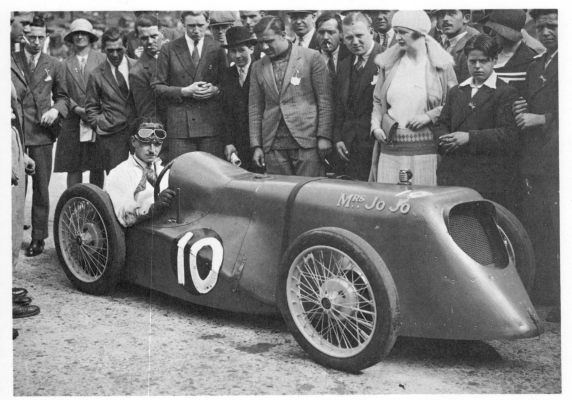

A good attempt at streamlining. H. C. Spero won several races with this car at Brooklands in 1928 and 1929.

Gunnar Poppe in a race car in road trim in the summer of 1929.

One of the great Austin Seven successes. S. C. H. Davis and the Earl of March after winning the BRDC 500-miles race at Brooklands in September, 1930. The average speed over six hours was 83.41 mph.

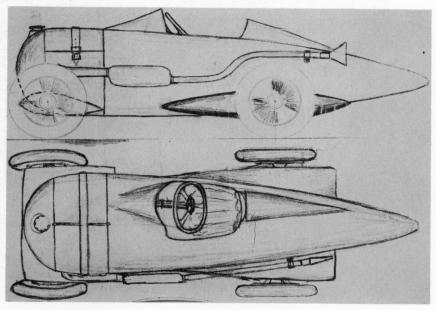

Sir Herbert's interest in racing car body design was revived in the early 1930's; this was his sketch for the 1931 supercharged works racer.

Three views of a car which was built along the lines of the sketch on the previous page in an attempt to capture records held by MGs at over 100 mph.

1637 miles at 68.24 mph was not good enough to beat the MGs in the Double-Twelve race in May, 1931. J. D. Barnes and Gunnar Poppe are pictured here against the backcloth of the Byfleet Banking at Brooklands.

A happier story. The orange 1931 500-miles race car with Leon Cushman and L. P. Driscoll after taking six Class H International records at Brooklands in October of that year. The car ran for three hours at 90.38 mph, for six hours at 90.12 mph, and covered 500 miles at 90.11 mph — a fantastic achievement at the time.

Sir Malcolm Campbell, the world land speed record holder, broke Class H records with this supercharged Austin Seven at Daytona Beach in February, 1931, averaging 94.06 mph for the mile and 93.96 mph for the kilometre.

Two mystery cars. Alf Depper at the wheel of a works Seven. When questioned in later years he could not recall any details.

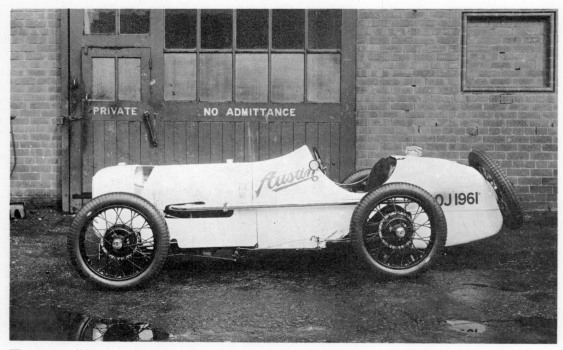

The note scribbled on the back of this photograph taken at the factory states merely "7 hp racer for Germany". Could it be one of the "Duck" racers?

The sporting Sevens

OL 166, the registration number used on one of the original racers, taking W. J. Milton to a silver cup in the Scottish Six-Day Trial in 1925.

For many years Austin Seven catalogues listed at least one production racer which was available to the public. This is the 1924 Gordon England Super Sports model, which was sold with a guaranteed speed of 80 mph.

HAVEN

Much slower, but just as attractive, this is the 1924 standard-model Sports Tourer.

Coveted by so many sporting motorists, the superb Ulster model. This example dates from 1931.

Two more views of the remarkable Ulster sports car.

Not quite so fast, but well suited for normal open-air motoring, this 1933/34 Sports 65 was known as the Nippy.

The last member of the standard production sports range of the following year, the Speedy.

The Twin-Cams

A twin-overhead-camshaft racer fully restored and now part of the Donington Collection.

The car in its hey-day, with Charlie Dodson hard at work in the cockpit.

The ohc racer's cockpit as it is displayed today at Donington.

Dodson celebrates after winning the 1938 British Empire Trophy race at an average of 70.57 mph.

Dodson beginning his record-breaking runs in October, 1936. He broke the Brooklands Outer Circuit class record at 121.14 mph and took nine records in all, including 100 miles at an average of 115.06 mph.

Murray Jamieson's twin-overhead-camshaft engine. His first Austin success had been with a streamlined side-valve supercharged car in which he captured records from MG in 1933.

A famous picture taken at the Nuffield Trophy race at Donington in July, 1936, with Bira (4) in side-valve and Goodacre (2), Dodson (6) and Driscoll (5) in ohc racers.

A closer view of Dodson's car at the pits.

The ohc racers were well-suited for hill-climbing, a branch of motor sport which achieved a high degree of popularity during the 1930's.

Adjusting his goggles, Bert Hadley about to make his fastest climb of Shelsley Walsh, in 40.05 seconds, in June, 1939. That year saw not only the last of the Austin Seven racing cars in action, but also the end of the Seven as a production car.

The Grasshoppers

One of four famous Austin Seven trials cars which had consecutive registration numbers and were active in rough-road events from 1936 to 1938. This is W. H. Scrivens on Litton Slack in the 1936 Buxton Trial.

C. D. Buckley makes easy work of Park Rash, in Yorkshire. The Grasshoppers were also said to have formed the basis of the four Austin entries at Le Mans in 1937.

A. H. Langley climbing The Yeld during the MG Car Club's 1938 Midland Sporting Trial. His Grasshopper earned him the Bryant Cup for the best performance of the day.

The fourth of the consecutive Grasshoppers tackling a rock-strewn climb in 1936.

Three more views, above, below and lower left, of the Grasshopper in its definitive form.

Sevens around the world

Snapped in Melbourne, Australia, in 1944, this well-preserved Seven was thought by its owner to be one of the 200-mile race cars.

Used by G. Smith for record-breaking in New Zealand in 1937, this single-seater set a new local one-mile record at 100.17 mph.

A sport of a very different kind; an Austin Seven used for a "Wall of Death" display in the mid-1930's.

A supercharged special in South Africa. This car was cleverly converted to independent front-wheel suspension by D. van Riet, who raced it successfully until 1939.

In 1929, Miss De Havilland took part in a sponsored drive around the world in this Austin Seven. Later, so many people wanted to repeat the journey at an advertiser's expense that encouragement to do so was soon withdrawn. . . . .

. . . . . But not before two New Zealanders, Hector MacQuarrie and Richard B. Matthews had made a similar journey in 1931. MacQuarrie, seen here shaking hands with Arthur Waite, Sir Herbert's son-in-law, later wrote a book about their adventure.

THE HANDY LITTLE CAR

Strictly commercial

This attractive fleet of Seven vans, used throughout Devon and Cornwall in 1933, was supplied by A. C. Turner, Austin's Plymouth agent.

The first Austin Seven commercial vehicle, built in 1923, offered a payload of 2¼ cwt. Several years were to pass before the market for an Austin light van was properly developed.

In 1938, the Royal Automobile Club of Victoria, Australia, bought these five smart vans for motor patrol and rescue work.

Despite its compact dimensions, the Austin Seven van offered considerable scope for sign-writers and artists. This is one of a fleet of Farm Ice Cream vans based in Yorkshire in 1932.

In 1937, Moreland's of Gloucester adapted this Seven for a midget for advertising purposes, using an earlier-model chassis and small wheels on which to mount a remarkably well-proportioned body.

The most successful Austin Seven commercial vehicle, the standard-model Ruby 5 cwt van.

The Seven engine in its final, 1938, form was used to power the first Reliant three-wheelers, which featured motorcycle-type front suspension grafted on to a suitably modified steering mechanism.

Many Austin Sevens were adapted for further use at the end of their motoring days; this example was used to drive a circular saw blade for another ten years.

Nostalgia

A final reminder of the hey-day of the Austin Seven

with a picture taken at the 1931 Motor Show in Milan.

OTHER BOOKS ON THE AUSTIN SEVEN

The Motor for the Million: The Austin Seven 1922–1939 (Wyatt)

'Motor Sport' Book of the Austin Seven (ed. Boddy)

Austin Seven Specials (Williams)

Seven Years with Samantha (Ball)

Austin Racing History (Harrison)

Austin Seven in the Thirties (magazine extracts)

Whatever Became of the Baby Austin (Underwood — USA)

(In addition to the above, certain reprinted Austin Seven
handbooks and spare parts lists are available through
specialist motoring booksellers.)

Further information on the above-listed titles
and on all special-interest motoring books
is available on request from
CONNOISSEUR CARBOOKS ADVISORY SERVICE
70 Chiswick High Road, London W4 1SY.